MY BIG BOOK OF
ANIMALS

Foreword by Gerald Durrell

Text by Helen Gilks and Ruth Thomson
Illustrated by Sharon Beeden, John Green
and Doreen McGuinness

Derrydale Books
New York

Foreword

When I was young I was very lucky as I lived on a beautiful island
in Greece, in a big house in the country. I have always been interested
in animals and so I could keep many different sorts of pets.
I had three dogs, pigeons, chickens, goats, a donkey called Sally
and a cow called Dulcie. But as well as these domestic
animals I had many wild pets such as beetles and butterflies,
tortoises, snakes, owls, hawks, canaries and many other
sorts of singing birds. My bedroom and the garden were full of animals
and in the morning when they all woke up the noise was
terrific with the dogs barking, cocks crowing, all the birds
singing, my donkey Sally going ''Hee-haw, hee-haw''
for her breakfast and Dulcie mooing to be taken out to the fields
so that she could graze on the fresh green grass. Sometimes my mother
said the animals were so noisy that she could not hear herself speak.
With my animal friends I had many lovely adventures. Sometimes I
would take a picnic and, riding on Sally and with my three dogs,
we would spend all day up in the hills, catching lizards and other creatures.
On other occasions we would go out in my boat which my brother had built
for me. We would catch all sorts of beautifully coloured fish
and crabs for my aquarium and swim in the warm blue sea.
As I grew older I decided I wanted a zoo of my own to keep many
different kinds of animals from all over the world.
Well, you can't build a zoo overnight. It took a lot of hard work and a lot
of money, but at last my dream came true and I have my zoo on the island
of Jersey in the Channel Islands. Here we have highly coloured
parrots from Africa and India, lots of different kinds of monkey – from the
huge black gorillas from Africa to tiny golden marmosets, smaller than
a kitten, from South America. We have tortoises, snow leopards, pink
flamingos and lots and lots of other animals besides.
I am very lucky that all my life I have had my animal friends around me,
as I think that studying animals is one of the most interesting things you can do.
From this lovely book you will learn a lot about many different
sorts of creature and their habits. I know you will like it and I hope
that when you grow up you will still love animals and
want to protect and help them wherever they are in the world.

Gerald Durrell

This 1991 edition published by
DERRYDALE Books,
distributed by Outlet Book Company, Inc.,
a Random House Company,
225 Park Avenue South, New York, New York 10003.

Printed and bound in Singapore

ISBN 0-517-051826
87654321

Cover: Giant Panda **Opposite:** Hippo

Contents

Polar bear

Polar bears come from icy lands, where they feed on fish and seals. Their fur and a thick layer of fat under their skin help to keep them warm.

Brown bear

Brown bears eat almost anything they can find – nuts, fruits, insects, fish, honey, and small animals. They sleep through some of the winter when food is more difficult to find.

Elephant

Elephants eat grass, leaves, and fruit. They pick up their food with their trunks. Elephants enjoy bathing. Young ones play squirting games with one another.

Chimpanzee

Chimpanzees live in family groups. The young ones stay with their mothers until they are four years old. They eat fruit, nuts, and, in the wild, dig for termites with sticks.

Lion

Lions are meat eaters. When they yawn, you can see their sharp teeth. The male lion is the one with the shaggy mane.

Tiger

Tigers eat meat as well. They catch their prey with their claws. They scratch their claws on trees to keep them sharp.

Camel

Camels come from hot, dry places. They can go for weeks without drinking. They have a store of fat – used as food – in their humps.

Llama

Llamas are found in mountainous places. They are very sure-footed. Mountain people use them to carry their heavy loads to and from market.

Giraffe

Giraffes are the tallest animals in the world. They nibble leaves and new branches of trees. See how they have to spread their long legs to drink.

Zebra

Zebras live in herds which graze on the plains of Africa.
They clean their coats by rolling in the dust.

Pelican

Pelicans have enormous pouched beaks for catching fish.
They swallow the fish whole.

Flamingo

Flamingos live in groups in shallow, salty water. When a flamingo eats, it puts its whole head in the water.

Macaw

Macaws are parrots. They can crack nuts with their strong beaks. They are very noisy and shriek very loudly.

Toucan

The toucan's long beak makes it easy for it to reach fruit in the wild. It takes the food with the tip of its beak and then throws back its head to toss the food down its throat.

Dolphin

Dolphins live in large groups, called schools, in warm seas. They are clever and very curious.

Penguin

Penguins cannot fly, but they are very good swimmers indeed. When they move on land, they waddle or hop. They feed on fish.

Duck

Ducks like water. If there is a pond, they will dunk for weeds and water creatures. They also eat grass and grain. Farmers may collect their eggs to eat.

Goose

Geese make good watchdogs. They honk loudly when people come near. Farm geese are too heavy to fly properly. They feed on grass and sometimes live in orchards.

Rooster

A rooster has beautiful feathers. He often crows loudly early in the morning. Roosters scratch and peck the ground for seeds and insects and the farmer also feeds them grain.

Hen

Hens lay eggs. If a hen can keep her eggs, she will sit on them until the chicks hatch. At night, the hens are shut inside to keep them safe from foxes.

Cat

Grain is dried and stored in barns or silos. Farmers often have cats to help keep mice and rats out of the farmyard and away from their grain. Farm cats usually live outside.

Goat

Farmers keep goats for their milk. Goats can climb and jump well. They like to eat all kinds of plants, even prickly ones. Baby goats are called kids.

Cow

A cow usually has one calf each year. The newborn calf is covered with hair. It can stand on its feet to drink milk from its mother very soon after it is born.

Calf

Calves are curious and playful. They sniff and lick strange objects. These calves have started to eat grass. Like fully grown cattle, they spend most of the time chewing.

Pig

These pigs live outside. They like to dig in the ground with their snouts, so their pen is often very muddy. In hot weather, they wallow in the mud to keep cool.

Rabbit

Rabbits nibble at many of the crops that are grown on different farms. Since the farmers have worked very hard planting, they try to keep the rabbits out of the fields.

Sheep

The mother sheep, or ewe, usually has her lambs in spring.
She may have one, two, or even three lambs. They are very
playful and run races and jump in the air.

Shearing

In summer, sheep do not need their thick, wool coats. The farmer shears off the wool with clippers. By winter, the sheep will have grown new coats to keep them warm.

Sheepdog

A shepherd often has a sheepdog to help round up the sheep, and move them from place to place. He whistles and makes arm signals to the dog to tell it what to do.

Pony

In the past, large, heavy horses were kept on farms to pull plows and carts. Nowadays, few are used for work, but horses and ponies are sometimes kept for riding.

Caterpillar

A caterpillar feeds on the leaves of plants and grows until, one day, it turns into a chrysalis or cocoon. Inside the cocoon a great change takes place.

Butterfly

The caterpillars have changed into beautiful butterflies and have come out of their cocoons. Watch them fly gracefully on sunny days. They visit flowers to drink the nectar.

Frog

Frogs have long, strong back legs to jump with. They like damp places and catch insects with their long tongues. In spring, look in ponds for their eggs.

Dragonfly

The dragonfly darts quickly about over water. It is a skillful hunter and can catch insects as it flies. It can even scoop them up from the water's surface as it flies.

Moth

Moths look like butterflies but most kinds fly only at night.
They are attracted to lights and often fly into houses.
During the day, moths hide on tree trunks and on plants.

Worm

Worms live in the ground, burrowing their way through the soil. At night, they may come above ground and search for leaves to eat. Can you see that they have no legs or eyes?

Spider

This garden spider spins a sticky web. It waits for a fly or a moth to get caught in the threads. Then it rushes out to capture it.

Ant

Ants live in nests. Follow a trail of ants and see where they live. Some of them are busy all day long gathering food. What are they taking back to their nest?

Bee

Honeybees and bumblebees buzz from flower to flower all summer long. They collect nectar and pollen to take to their nests. Can you see the pollen basket on this honeybee's leg?

42

Wasp

Wasps also feed on nectar, but they eat insects and fruit as well. These wasps live together in a large papery nest. They have a sharp stinger to defend themselves.

Snail

Snails come out in wet weather or at night to eat plants. During the day, they usually hide away inside their shells. Follow their silvery trails to find where they hide.

Slug

Slugs are like snails, but they do not have shells to hide in. Instead, they burrow into the ground or hide under a stone. They come out at night or after rain, to feed on plants.

Beetle

This is a ground beetle. It can run quickly on its long legs and it hunts for food at night. Although this one stays on the ground, most other types of beetle have wings and can fly.

Ladybug

Ladybugs are a type of beetle. They eat the greenfly which spoils our roses. Not all types of ladybug have the same number of spots. How many does this one have?

Sparrow

In spring and summer, sparrows are busy collecting food for their hungry young. The nests are well hidden and in winter the sparrows use them for shelter.